D1442017

A Muslim Family's Chair for the Pope

A true story from
Bosnia & Herzegovina

Stefan Salinas

Camelopardalis
SAN FRANCISCO

In memory of one of the more exquisite flowers
in God's garden,

Rose Abdelnour Zimbardo

The wood-carved designs in this book were all drawn from works by the Hajder-Art Studio.
   You can learn more about their artistry at: **www.hajder-art.com**
A very special thank you to those who helped make this book possible:
   Edževit Winkler-Žepčanin, Salim & Edin Hajderovac, Hidajeta Alic & Senad Osmanovic,
And the proofreaders: Sabrina DeCarolis, Imam Hafiz Khalid Siddiqi, Fr. Michael Strange, S.S.
   & William Dohar. *Folks full of heart* ♥ *Your assistance was a true blessing!*
Thanks to Ismar Poric of Superar Srebrenica, Will T. Golden, Fr. Tony LaTorre, Colin
   & to my family & friends for their love & support.

ISBN-10: 0-9986088-0-7 ISBN-13: 978-0-9986088-0-8
Library of Congress Control Number: 2017900563

Printed on acid-free paper by IngramSpark, USA/UK/Australia   First edition January 2017.
   Artwork: Color pencil, ink & acrylic on Neenah Environment Desert Storm paper.
   Fonts: Georgia, Adobe Arabic & Century Schoolbook.

Camelopardalis / Stefan Salinas, PO Box 470041, San Francisco, CA USA 94147
www.stefansalinas.com

Hello, my name is Salim Hajderovac.
I am a carpenter, just like my father, and just like
my two sons, Edin and Benjamin.

My father was Haji Sulejman Hajderovac.
He opened this woodshop over fifty years ago.
I have kept the trade up, along with my son Edin.

I live with my wife in the small town of Zavidovici,
in the European country called Bosnia and Herzegovina.

Benjamin moved to Germany, but he returns now and again to help us out.

What are
we busy making,
do you ask?

All sorts of things,
for homes,
hotels,
restaurants,
cafés...

We carve tables,
mirror frames,
fireplace mantles,
chairs,
containers,
signs,

...all out of wood.

We also make objects to help people worship God. Plaques with words from the Qur'an

hang in Muslim homes, mosques and Muslim monasteries (*tekkes*).

My family and I are Muslims,

but we also carve pictures of saints for Orthodox Christian and Catholic homes and churches.

We also make crucifixes
and souvenirs for the thousands of pilgrims that travel to
Our Lady of Medjugorje Catholic Shrine,
three hours south of here.

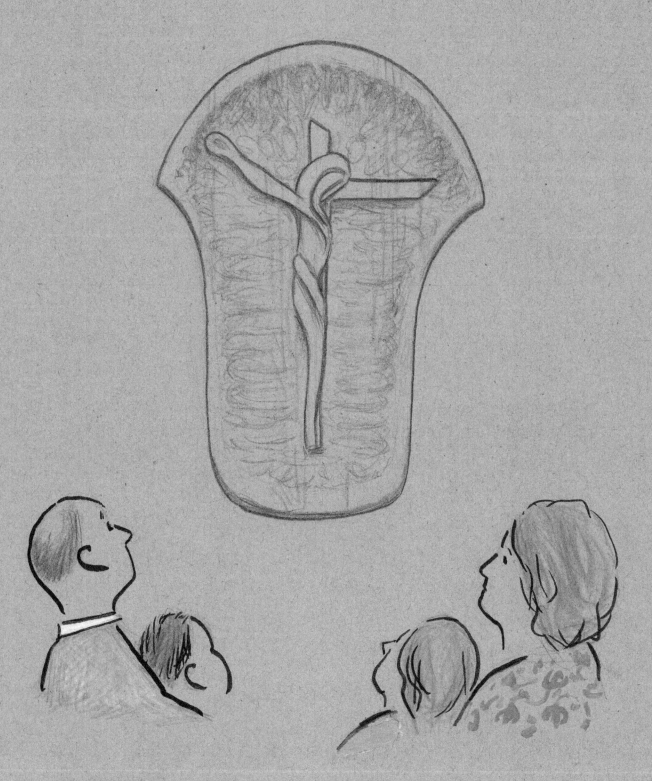

Christians believe that Jesus Christ (peace be upon him) was the son of God, and that he is the Savior of the World.

In Islam, Jesus is seen as a prophet. Muslims learn about Allah (God)
from the teachings of the Prophet Muhammad (peace be upon him).

Here in Zavidovici, most of us
get along with one another,
as we have for generations.

Sadly,
in my country,
Christians and Muslims
have not always
been friends.

Sadly,
in the wider world,
there are too many examples
of hatred and fighting
between people of
different faiths.

One evening during dinnertime, there was
an announcement on TV:

"On June 6, 2015, Pope Francis,
    the head of the Catholic Church,
    is going to visit Bosnia and Herzegovina."

Immediately, in my head appeared an image
of a chair for the Pope, and I was its creator!

There is a tradition in some countries of making a chair for visiting popes.
It is a welcoming gesture.
You must understand, this new pope is respected by people from many
backgrounds, for he reaches out to everyone with a message of peace.

I quickly began sketching.

The next day, I showed the final drawings to my good friend
Father Miro Beslic, who is the pastor of St. Joseph's,
the Catholic church in town.

He liked the idea and faxed it over to Cardinal Vinko Puljic,
leader of the Catholics in Bosnia.

The Cardinal sent the sketches to Rome, and three days later,
over all the other submissions, my design was approved!

I was in shock. For ten days, I walked around stunned in disbelief.

Wake up Salim, it's your turn to play!

In the City Mosque of Zavidovici, during our Friday
Jumu'ah prayer,
we said: الله أكبر "God is Great."

And I thought, *Allah, am I going too far?*

Our leader, Imam Izet Čamdžić, recited,

يُسَبِّحُ لِلَّهِ مَا فِي السَّمَاوَاتِ وَمَا فِي الْأَرْضِ الْمَلِكِ الْقُدُّوسِ الْعَزِيزِ الْحَكِيمِ

بِسْمِ اللَّهِ وَجَلَّ شَأْنُهُ الْمَسْجِدِ الْأَقْصَى

"All that is in the heavens and the Earth
glorifies Allah, the King, the Holy,
the Almighty, the Wise."

And I thought, *As a Muslim
making a chair for
the Catholic pope,
am I crazy?*

We turned to our right, then turned to our left, saying:

السلام عليكم ورحمة الله وبركاته

"Peace and the mercy of Allah be upon you."

And I thought, *This historic visit is very important for my neighbors...*

Sometimes the Pope is called the *Pontiff*, which comes from the Latin word *pontifex*, which means "bridge builder".

By making this gift for Pontiff Francis, perhaps I am building a bridge between my community and theirs.

One day, Father Miro and I drove over to Sarajevo,
our country's capital city. We went to meet with Cardinal Vinko
and the organizers for the Pope's visit. Everyone present made
suggestions for the chair's design. It was a collaborative effort.

Father Miro made an appeal to his flock, asking for them to raise money to pay for the materials

(walnut is expensive!).

Edin and I donated our time.

We sharpened our carving knives
and laid out our tools for the
  great task before us.
A strict schedule was drawn up.
All other wood orders were put on
hold, for we had only three short
  months to create the chair.
A fellow carpenter brought over cut
  lumber pieces.

I called my son Benjamin. He flew over from Germany to help us.

Other friends joined in the effort.
Imam Izet and my Muslim community
  were very supportive.

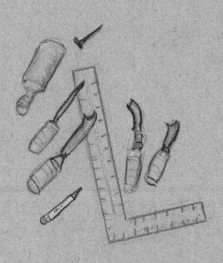

To our surprise, reporters poured into our tiny workshop.

News of our project spread around our city, then our country, then the world!
We were on the internet, on television, and in newspapers.

Radio
Slobodna
Evropa

ALJAZEERA

Libération

L'Orient
LE JOUR

Oumma.com

tV1

V·A
Voice of America

AFP

BBC
WORLD
SERVICE

klix

Le Point.fr

Diario
EL ARGENTINO

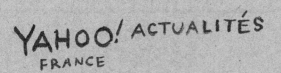

YAHOO! ACTUALITÉS
FRANCE

And now for
the design.

We carved fish in the chair's arms,
for the fish is a symbol the first Christians
used to identify themselves.

In the Christian's holy book, the Bible,
it is written that Jesus,
performed a miracle,

taking a few fish and loaves of bread
and multiplying them to feed a gathering
of five thousand people.

In their book, Jesus said,

> "I am the Alpha and the Omega,
> the First and the Last, the Beginning and the End."

The first letter of the Greek
alphabet is the *Alpha*,

A

and the last letter
is the *Omega*.

Ω

There are wavy designs known as *wattle*, and they can be found on early Catholic stone buildings and structures, some dating back hundreds of years.

A Catholic worship service is called a *Mass*.

During a Mass, the priest presents to the people bread and wine, which they believe becomes the body and blood of Jesus Christ.

Bread is made from wheat, and wine is made from grapes.

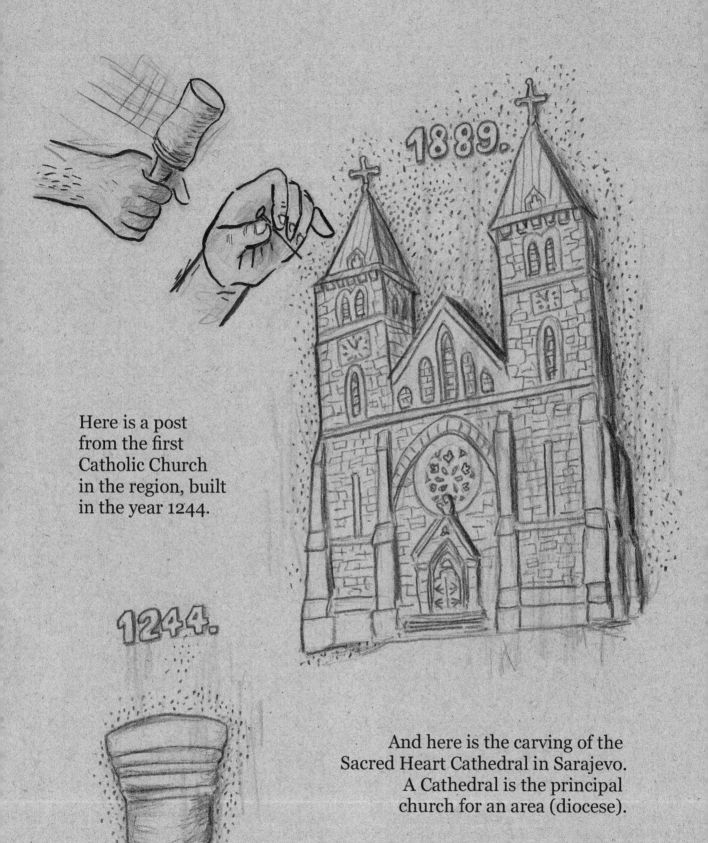

1889.

Here is a post
from the first
Catholic Church
in the region, built
in the year 1244.

1244.

And here is the carving of the
Sacred Heart Cathedral in Sarajevo.
A Cathedral is the principal
church for an area (diocese).

Of course we had to acknowledge
my friend's church on the chair.

Father Miro saw this and smiled
   from ear to ear!

On the back
of the chair is
Pope Francis'
Coat of Arms,

a symbol of
who he is and where
he comes from.

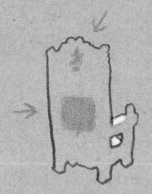

To announce the Pope's visit, a logo was made by the graphic designers Miroslav Selka and Dragan Ivanovic.

"Mir vama" means "Peace to you" in Bosnian.

Work, eat, pray, sleep. Work, eat, pray, sleep. Work, eat pray, sleep. Work, eat, pray, sleep... *Whew!* We were busy!

Cardinal Vinko and Monsignor Tomo Knežević stopped in
to check on our progress. They were very pleased.

Less than a month
  to our deadline,
  it began to rain.

It was the day before
Lailat al Mi'raj, the night
we celebrate the journey
Muhammad took up to the
heavens to learn how to pray
from Allah and the prophets.

I encountered a weeping woman,
and I asked her,
  "Why are you crying?"

She replied,
  "I am remembering my
    brothers and sisters
    who died during the war."

Water was pouring down from the sky. It rained during the night and through the next day. It rained and rained and rained...

Mud slid down from the hills,
and the Bosnia river
waters rose,

and flooded
into people's homes,

into people's
shops,

and
even into
the tiny mosque
uptown.

The waters tore
the Rainbow Bridge
from its foot-hold,

and it floated
downstream...

Finally, the rains let up, and all of the townspeople worked together to clean up and begin to rebuild Zavidovici.

... And we had a chair to finish!

We stained the wood to protect it, and then attached soft, white cushions. Our project took over two thousand hours to complete.

Here is the chair.

Edin and I brought the chair
to St. Joseph's Church,
to present it to the parish
that paid for it.

I explained the symbols adorning it and
I thanked them for their support.

It was time to wrap it up
and transport it to Sarajevo.
Police cars safely escorted
us all the way.

The cathedral was too small for the expected number of people, so the Asim Ferhatović Hase Stadium was transformed for the Mass. Chairs were set out and a stage for the sanctuary was made.

Pope Francis arrived to a cheering crowd at the airport.

He met with the members of Bosnia's presidency.

He met with youths,

and the Superar Srebrenica children's choir sang for him, "Love people, love people."

He spoke with the Bosnian religious leaders from Islam, Christianity and Judaism.

But the biggest event was the Mass he conducted at the stadium,

which was filled
with ten thousand people!

The Pope prayed,

he preached,

he broke bread,

and during certain parts of the Mass, he sat in that chair.

My family and I were standing in the first row. We were honored to be there.

Our family and
friends were so happy for us!
Here ends my story of how a chair
for Pope Francis was made in Bosnia and Herzegovina.

CPSIA information can be obtained
at www.ICGtesting.com
Printed in the USA
LVOW02*0807080917

547989LV00006B/13/P